How To Use This Study Guide

This five-lesson study guide corresponds to *"There's More to You Than Meets the Eye" With Rick Renner* **(Renner TV)**. Each lesson in this study guide covers a topic that is addressed during the program series, with questions and references supplied to draw you deeper into your own private study of the Scriptures on this subject.

To derive the most benefit from this study guide, consider the following:

First, watch or listen to the program prior to working through the corresponding lesson in this guide. (Programs can also be viewed at **renner.org** by clicking on the Media/Archives links or on our Renner Ministries YouTube channel.)

Second, take the time to look up the scriptures included in each lesson. Prayerfully consider their application to your own life.

Third, use a journal or notebook to make note of your answers to each lesson's Study Questions and Practical Application challenges.

Fourth, invest specific time in prayer and in the Word of God to consult with the Holy Spirit. Write down the scriptures or insights He reveals to you.

Finally, take action! Whatever the Lord tells you to do according to His Word, do it.

For added insights on this subject, it is recommended that you obtain Kenneth E. Hagin's book *Growing Up Spiritually*. You may also select from Rick's other available resources by placing your order at **renner.org** or by calling 1-800-742-5593.

TOPIC

There's More to You Than Meets the Eye

SCRIPTURES

1. **1 Thessalonians 5:23** — And the very God of peace sanctify you wholly; and I pray God your whole spirit and soul and body be preserved blameless unto the coming of our Lord Jesus Christ.

2. **John 3:1-7** — There was a man of the Pharisees, named Nicodemus, a ruler of the Jews: The same came to Jesus by night, and said unto him, Rabbi, we know that thou art a teacher come from God: for no man can do these miracles that thou doest, except God be with him. Jesus answered and said unto him, Verily, verily, I say unto thee, Except a man be born again, he cannot see the kingdom of God. Nicodemus saith unto him, How can a man be born when he is old? can he enter the second time into his mother's womb, and be born? Jesus answered, Verily, verily, I say unto thee, Except a man be born of water and of the Spirit, he cannot enter into the kingdom of God. That which is born of the flesh is flesh; and that which is born of the Spirit is spirit. Marvel not that I said unto thee, Ye [all of you] must be born again.

GREEK WORDS

1. "sanctify" — ἁγιάζω (*hagiadzo*): to sanctify, to set apart, or to consecrate as holy

2. "wholly" — ὁλοτελής (*holoteles*): a compound of ὅλος (*holos*) and τέλος (*telos*); the word ὅλος (*holos*) means every single part and pictures all the parts working together in sync; the word τέλος (*telos*) depicts completion or maturity; compounded, it describes fully layered parts

3. "whole" — ὁλόκληρος (*holokleros*): a compound of ὅλος (*holos*) and κλῆρος (*kleros*); the word ὅλος (*holos*) means every single part and pictures all the parts working together in sync; the word κλῆρος (*kleros*) is the word for an inheritance or what is assigned to a person;

compounded, it refers to what is assigned and given to each person; complete, entire, or whole in all respects

4. "spirit" — **τὸ πνεῦμα** (*to pneuma*): with a definite article, the spirit; the life force of a person; one's core; one's real self; the eternal part of a person

5. "soul" — **ἡ ψυχὴ** (*he psuche*): with a definite article, the soul; the mind, will, and emotions; the mind is the control center; where we get the words psyche and psychology

6. "body" — **τὸ σῶμα** (*to soma*): with a definite article, the body; refers to the human body

7. "born again" — **γεννηθῇ ἄνωθεν** (*gennethe anothen*): born from above; a second, heavenly, spiritual, supernatural birth

8. "born of water" — **ἐξ ὕδατος** (*ex hudatos*): out of water; a natural birth; when a mother's water breaks; thus, a first, natural birth out of water

9. "of the Spirit" — **καὶ Πνεύματος** (*kai Pneumatos*): of or by the Spirit

10. "cannot" — **οὐ δύναται** (*ou dunatai*): it is not possible

11. "the kingdom" — **τὴν βασιλείαν** (*ten basileian*): definite article with a form of **βασιλεία** (*basileia*); dominion, kingdom; rule; by necessity, it is a kingdom with a king; when used with a definite article in the New Testament, it denotes the kingdom rule of God and of Christ

12. "of the flesh is flesh" — **ἐκ τῆς σαρκὸς, σάρξ ἐστιν** (*ek tes sarkos, sarx estin*): out of the flesh, flesh is

13. "of the Spirit is spirit" — **ἐκ τοῦ Πνεύματος, πνεῦμά ἐστιν** (*ek tou Pneumatos, pneuma estin*) out of or by the Spirit, spirit is

14. "marvel not" — **μὴ θαυμάσῃς** (*me thaumase*s): the particle **μή** (*me*) makes this a prohibition; used with a form of the word **θαυμάζω** (*thaumadzo*), which means to wonder, to be at a loss of words, to be shocked and amazed; bewildered; as a phrase, it means do not be amazed, do not be shocked, do not be bewildered

15. "must" — **δεῖ** (*dei*): an absolute necessity

16. "Ye [all of you]" — **ὑμᾶς** (*humas*): here translated all, but it is plural, referring to everyone; thus, this is a requirement for all with no exceptions

17. "born again" — **γεννηθῆναι ἄνωθεν** (*gennethenai anothen*): born from above; a second, heavenly, spiritual, supernatural birth

SYNOPSIS

The five lessons in this study titled *There's More to You Than Meets the Eye* will focus on the following topics:

- There's More to You Than Meets the Eye

- The Spirit: The Real You at the Core of Your Being

- The Mind: The Central Control Center of Your Life

- The Body: The House Where You Live, the Instrument God Gave You

- Let God Touch Every Layer of Your Life

Have you ever seen a Russian Matryoshka doll? It is a whimsical figurine that has multiple dolls inside it. Sometimes referred to as a nesting doll, the Russian Matryoshka doll comes in all shapes and sizes and is an excellent illustration of the multi-layered being that we are. God created us as a spirit being and we have a soul and we live in a body. Indeed, there is more to us than meets the eye!

The emphasis of this lesson:

What you see when you look at yourself in the mirror is not all there is. You are a tri-part being — you are a spirit who has a soul and lives in a body. When you got saved, your spirit was made totally new, and the work God did in your spirit is the same work He desires to do in every part of you.

God Wants To 'Sanctify' Every Part of Us

Probably the greatest verse in the New Testament to demonstrate our multi-layered makeup is First Thessalonians 5:23. Writing under the inspiration of the Holy Spirit, the apostle Paul said, "And the very God of peace sanctify you wholly; and I pray God your whole spirit and soul and body be preserved blameless unto the coming of our Lord Jesus Christ."

Many people hear the words "soul" and "spirit" and think they are synonymous, but they are not, as we will continue to see in this series. Each part of our being is uniquely different and has a very specific function. Paul began by saying, "And the very God of peace *sanctify* you *wholly...*" (1 Thessalonians 5:23).

The word "sanctify" here is a form of the Greek word *hagiadzo*, which means *to sanctify*, *to set apart*, or *to consecrate as holy*. God wants to sanctify you and set you apart to Himself, and He wants to do it "wholly." This word "wholly" is the Greek word *holoteles*, a compound of *holos* and *telos*. The word *holos* means *every single part* and pictures *all the parts working together in sync*. The word *telos* depicts *completion* or *maturity*. When we compound these words to form *holoteles*, it describes *something that is fully layered and has multiple parts*.

As human beings created in the image of God, we are fully layered and made up of multiple parts — spirit, soul, and body. And God wants to sanctify every layer of who we are. That is what Paul went on to say in First Thessalonians 5:23. He said, "…I pray God your whole spirit and soul and body be preserved blameless unto the coming of our Lord Jesus Christ."

Notice the word "whole" — the Greek word *holokleros*. It is a compound of the words *holos* and *kleros*. The word *holos*, again, means *every single part* and pictures *all the parts working together in sync*; and the word *kleros* is the word for *an inheritance* or *what is assigned to a person*. When compounded, the word *holokleros* refers to *what God has assigned and given to each person*. Regardless of ethnicity, background, age, or gender, each one of us has been given a spirit, soul, and body.

We Are 'Spirit, Soul, and Body'

According to God's Word, we are a "spirit, soul, and body" being. The word "spirit" in First Thessalonians 5:23 is *to pneuma* in Greek. It is the word *pneuma* with a definite article, meaning *the spirit*. It describes *the life force of a person*; *one's core*, or *one's real self*. It is *the core eternal part of each one of us*.

Along with being an eternal spirit, we also have a *soul*. This word "soul" in First Thessalonians 5:23 is translated from *he psuche* in Greek, and like the word "spirit," it, too, appears with a definite article, which indicates *the soul*. The interesting thing about the soul is that it's also made up of layers — the *mind*, *will*, and *emotions*. Clearly, the mind is the control center of our life. It's also interesting to note that the word *psuche* is where we get the words "psyche" and "psychology."

The third aspect of our tri-part being is the "body." This is a translation of the Greek words *to soma*. Like the spirit and soul, the word "body" also appears with a definite article, meaning, simply, *the body*, and it refers to *the human body*. Every human being has been assigned a spirit, a soul, and a body, and all three parts are supposed to work in sync — or in harmony — with each other.

The Spirit Must Be 'Born Again'

Before surrendering our life to the lordship of Jesus, all of us "…were dead in trespasses and sins" (Ephesians 2:1). Through faith in Jesus' finished work of redemption on the Cross, we can be made alive in Him and transferred out of the kingdom of darkness into the Kingdom of light (*see* Colossians 1:13). This is what Jesus described as being *born again*.

The Bible says, "There was a man of the Pharisees, named Nicodemus, a ruler of the Jews: The same came to Jesus by night, and said unto him, Rabbi, we know that thou art a teacher come from God: for no man can do these miracles that thou doest, except God be with him. Jesus answered and said unto him, Verily, verily, I say unto thee, Except a man be *born again*, he cannot see the kingdom of God" (John 3:1-3).

Take note of the phrase "born again." It is a translation of the Greek words *gennethe anothen*, which literally mean *born from above*. This phrase refers to *a divine, heavenly, supernatural birth that comes from God above*. Here we see Jesus begin to use comparative language, as He compares natural physical birth into the human race with spiritual birth into the Kingdom of God.

Greatly puzzled by Jesus' words, Nicodemus responded logically, and asked Him, "…How can a man be born when he is old? can he enter the second time into his mother's womb, and be born? Jesus answered, Verily, verily, I say unto thee, Except a man be born of water and of the Spirit, he cannot enter into the kingdom of God" (John 3:4,5).

What did Jesus mean when He said we must be "born of water"? This phrase is a translation of the Greek words *ex hudatos*, which mean *out of water* and refer to *a natural birth*. When a woman is about to give birth to her baby, the amniotic sac, which is the fluid-filled sac that surrounds and protects the fetus, breaks. Thus, being "born of water" refers to the natural human birth that must take place in a person's life.

What did Jesus mean when He said we must be "born of the Spirit"? In Greek, the phrase "of the Spirit" is *kai Pneumatos*, which literally means *of* or *by the Spirit*. So in this powerful passage, Jesus identifies that there are two births: one is out of water, or a natural birth from a mother, and the other is *of the Spirit* or *by the Spirit of God* and is a spiritual birth. Jesus said that unless a person experiences both of these births, he *cannot* enter into the Kingdom of God.

The word "cannot" here is from the Greek words *ou dunatai*, and means *it is not possible*. Unless we are born from above by the Spirit of God, it is impossible for us to enter the Kingdom of God. In Greek, "the kingdom" is *ten basileian*, which contains the definite article *ten* along with a form of *basileia* (kingdom). Because the definite article is included, it describes *the dominion*, *the kingdom*, or *the rule of God*. By necessity, it is a kingdom with a king, and when it is used with a definite article in the New Testament, it denotes *the kingdom rule of God and of Christ*.

To be clear, there is no admittance into the Kingdom of God unless you experience both these births. Obviously, the first birth is when you are born of water and enter the human race. But to enter the Kingdom of Heaven, you must also be birthed from above — that is, you must be born again and experience the *supernatural* birth, which is by the Spirit.

Flesh Can Only Produce Flesh — It Is the Spirit That Produces Spirit

Jesus went on to tell Nicodemus, "That which is born of the flesh is flesh; and that which is born of the Spirit is spirit" (John 3:6). In Greek, the phrase "of the flesh is flesh" is *ek tes sarkos, sarx estin*, which literally means *out of the flesh, flesh is*. In other words, flesh produces flesh. A flesh-and-blood father and mother can only produce a flesh-and-blood baby.

However, "…That which is born of the Spirit is spirit" (John 3:6). The phrase "of the Spirit is spirit" — *ek tou Pneumatos, pneuma estin* in Greek — means *out of* or *by the Spirit, spirit is*. It is only by the Spirit of God that a person's spirit can be recreated in Christ Jesus. When we repent of sin and invite Jesus to be our Lord and Savior, it is our spirit that is born again — not our mind, not our emotions, and not our body.

Jesus then declared, "*Marvel not* that I said unto thee, Ye must be born again" (John 3:7). The words "marvel not" are a translation of the Greek phrase *me thaumases*. The particle *me* makes this *a prohibition*, and it is used with a form of the word *thaumadzo*, which means *to wonder* or *to be at a loss for words*. It carries the idea of being *shocked*, *amazed*, or *bewildered*. In the context here, *me thaumases* — translated as "marvel not" — means *do not be amazed, do not be shocked, do not be bewildered.*

Jesus told Nicodemus — and all of us — not to be shocked or amazed by Him saying, "…*Ye must* be born again" (John 3:7). The word "must" here is the Greek word *dei*, which always describes *an absolute necessity or obligation.* And the word "ye" in Greek is plural, meaning *all of you* or *everyone, no exceptions.* Thus, we could translate Jesus' words here as (in order to see the Kingdom of God), "…It is an absolute necessity that you and every member of the human race, with no exceptions, be born again."

Once more, we see the words "born again" — the Greek words *gennethenai anothen* — which mean *born from above* and describe *a second, heavenly, spiritual, supernatural birth.* Friend, the moment you got saved, your spirit was made completely new and totally like Jesus. You became one with Him and were clothed in His righteousness. Your spirit was recreated free of all defects, and there is absolutely nothing you can do to improve its condition.

"But what about my mind and body?" you ask. "Why do I still struggle at times with wrong thoughts and wrong behaviors if I'm born again?" The answer is that your soul and body were not re-created at salvation — only your spirit. It is the Spirit of God, through the Word of God, that works in and with us throughout our lifetime to renew our soul, which affects our body. That's why Paul prayed that "…the very God of peace sanctify you wholly; and I pray God your whole spirit and soul and body be preserved blameless unto the coming of our Lord Jesus Christ" (1 Thessalonians 5:23).

In the coming lessons, we will carefully unpack each of these aspects of who we are and see how they interact with each other. In our next lesson, we will specifically focus on the spirit, which is the life force of our being that, for the Christian, has been born again from above.

STUDY QUESTIONS

> **Study to shew thyself approved unto God, a workman that needeth not to be ashamed, rightly dividing the word of truth.**
> **— 2 Timothy 2:15**

1. Carefully read First Thessalonians 4:3-8. What does this passage say
    God's will is for your life? What does a "sanctified life" look like?
    What does an "unsanctified life" look like?

2. According to First Peter 1:2 and First Thessalonians 5:23 and 24,
    who specifically does the work of sanctification in your life?
    What extraordinary tool has God given you to sanctify your life?
    (*See* John 15:3; 17:17; Ephesians 5:26; and Psalm 119:9).
    Are you embracing and using this tool?

PRACTICAL APPLICATION

But be ye doers of the word, and not hearers only,
deceiving your own selves.
—James 1:22

1. Have you ever read Jesus' conversation with Nicodemus in John 3:1-21?
    If so, what did you understand Him to mean when He said, "…Except a
    man be born of water and of the Spirit, he cannot enter into the king-
    dom of God" (John 3:5)? How has this lesson expanded your under-
    standing of being born again?

2. Do you remember what took place the day you were saved? Where
    were you? Who did God use to lead you to Jesus? What details are
    most memorable about your salvation experience?

3. Jesus said, "Flesh gives birth to flesh, but the Spirit gives birth to spirit"
    (John 3:6 *NIV*). What does this tell you about trying to birth — or
    make something happen — in your own "fleshly" ability? In order for
    you to experience something godly and of eternal value, what has to
    take place? (Consider Abraham and Sarah's actions in Genesis 16:1-16;
    18:9-15; 21:1-21.)

TOPIC

The Spirit: The Real You at the Core of Your Being

SCRIPTURES

1. **1 Thessalonians 5:23** — And the very God of peace sanctify you wholly; and I pray God your whole spirit and soul and body be preserved blameless unto the coming of our Lord Jesus Christ.

2. **John 1:12,13** — But as many as received him, to them gave he power to become the sons of God, even to them that believe on his name: Which were born, not of blood, nor of the will of the flesh, nor of the will of man, but of God [were born].

3. **1 Corinthians 6:17** — But he that is joined unto the Lord is one spirit.

4. **2 Corinthians 5:17** — Therefore if any man be in Christ, he is a new creature: old things are passed away; behold, all things are become new.

5. **Romans 8:16** (*ESV*) — The Spirit himself bears witness with our spirit that we are children of God.

6. **James 2:26** (*ESV*) — For as the body apart from the spirit is dead....

7. **2 Corinthians 5:8** — We are confident, I say, and willing rather to be absent from the body, and to be present with the Lord.

8. **1 Corinthians 14:14-16** — For if I pray in an unknown tongue, my spirit prayeth, but my understanding is unfruitful. What is it then? I will pray with the spirit, and I will pray with the understanding also: I will sing with the spirit, and I will sing with the understanding also. Else when thou shalt bless with the spirit....

9. **2 Corinthians 4:16** — For which cause we faint not; but though our outward man perish, yet the inward man is renewed day by day.

GREEK WORDS

1. "sanctify" — ἁγιάζω (*hagiadzo*): to sanctify, to set apart, or to consecrate as holy

2. "wholly" — **ὁλοτελής** (*holoteles*): a compound of **ὅλος** (*holos*) and **τέλος** (*telos*); the word **ὅλος** (*holos*) means every single part and pictures all the parts working together in sync; the word **τέλος** (*telos*) depicts completion or maturity; compounded, it describes fully layered parts

3. "spirit" — **τὸ πνεῦμα** (*to pneuma*): with a definite article, the spirit; the life force of a person; one's core; one's real self; the eternal part of a person

4. "soul" — **ἡ ψυχὴ** (*he psuche*): with a definite article, the soul; the mind, will, and emotions; the mind is the control center; where we get the words psyche and psychology

5. "body" — **τὸ σῶμα** (*to soma*): with a definite article, the body; refers to the human body

6. "but" — **δέ** (*de*): an exclamatory statement; intended to get attention

7. "as many" — **ὅσος** (*hosos*): as great as; as much as; an unlimited number

8. "received" — **λαμβάνω** (*lambano*): to seize or lay hold of something in order to make it your own; to grab, capture, or take possession; one who graciously receives something that is freely and easily given

9. "power" — **ἐξουσία** (*exousia*): influence; delegated authority

10. "to become" — **γίνομαι** (*ginomai*): an initiated change that leads to a transition of one thing to another

11. "sons" — **τέκνον** (*teknon*): children who are still under parental guidance at home; children under the authority of a guardian

12. "on" — **εἰς** (*eis*): into; carries the idea of a merger

13. "not of blood" — **οὐκ ἐξ αἱμάτων** (*ouk ex haimaton*): not out of blood; not from blood

14. "nor of the will of the flesh" — **οὐδὲ ἐκ θελήματος σαρκὸς** (*oude ek thelematos sarkos*): neither out of the will of flesh; neither by the will of flesh

15. "nor of the will of man" — **οὐδὲ ἐκ θελήματος ἀνδρὸς** (*oude ek thelematos andros*): neither of the will of man; neither by the will of man

16. "but" — **ἀλλά** (*alla*): but on the other hand; intended to make a comparison

17. "of God [were born]" — **ἐκ Θεοῦ ἐγεννήθησαν** (*ek Theou egennethesan*): out of God were born; by God were born

18. "joined" — **κολλώμενος** (*kollomenos*): being joined; to adhere, to cleave, to join, or to be glued

19. "one spirit" — ἓν πνεῦμά ἐστιν (*hen pneuma estin*): one spirit; one with the Lord

20. "in Christ" — ἐν Χριστῷ (*en Christo*): literally, in Christ; located in Christ; in the sphere of Christ

21. "new" — καινός (*kainos*): new; brand new; freshly new; not a new version of something old, but brand spanking new

22. "creature" — κτίσις (*ktisis*): creation; something made from nothing; hence, not made with old materials, but something that never previously existed

23. "old things" — τὰ ἀρχαῖα (*ta archaia*): the archaic things; the old things; past things

24. "passed away" — παρέρχομαι (*parerchomai*): past; rendered void; null and void; to be disregarded; to be ignored

25. "behold" — ἰδού (*idou*): bewilderment, shock, amazement, and wonder

26. "bears witness" — συμμαρτυρέω (*summartureo*): witnesses together with

27. "absent" — ἐκδημέω (*ekdemeo*): to be away from home; hence, the human body is the home of the human spirit

28. "my spirit" — τὸ πνεῦμά μου (*to pneuma mou*): the spirit of me; my spirit

29. "with the spirit" — τῷ πνεύματι (*to pneumati*): with the human spirit

30. "with the understanding" — τῷ νοΐ (*to noi*): with the human mind; with the intellect; in the language of the mind

31. "[sing] with the spirit" — τῷ πνεύματι (*to pneumati*): with the human spirit

32. "[sing] with the understanding" — τῷ νοΐ (*to noi*): with the human mind; with the intellect; in the language of the mind

33. "with the spirit" — ἐν πνεύματι (*en pneumati*): in the human spirit; in the realm of the human spirit

34. "outward man" — ὁ ἔξω ἡμῶν ἄνθρωπος (*ho exo hemon anthropos*): the exterior man; our exterior self; the human body

35. "perish" — διαφθείρω (*diaphtheiro*): depicts what suffers the effects of wear, tear, and age

36. "inward man" — ὁ ἔσω ἡμῶν (*ho eso hemon*): the inner part of us; referring to the born-again human spirit

37. "renewed" — ἀνακαινόω (*anakainoo*): renewed again and again; hence, endlessly fresh, new, and unaffected by the effects of wear, tear, and age

SYNOPSIS

For many years, millions of tourists have come to Russia and purchased the unique crafts that originated within its borders. The handmade Russian Matryoshka doll is one such craft, and one of the most interesting things about these dolls is that when craftsmen make them, they start by creating the smallest-sized doll first. Once the very core doll is created, each successive-sized doll is then fashioned from the inside out until the nested doll is completed.

To a degree, each of us is like one of these Russian Matryoshka dolls. We have multiple layers to who we are, and the very core of our being is what God creates first. Deep down inside you is the *real* you — your human spirit. It serves as the life force of your being and is designed by God to live forever. Without the spirit, there is no life (*see* James 2:26). So, how do we develop our spirit?

The emphasis of this lesson:

The invitation to be born again from above is available to anyone who receives Christ by faith. The moment a person is saved, their human spirit is instantly perfected and becomes one with Jesus. Immediately, they are adopted as a son or daughter of God and are made a new creation. It is with our human spirit that we talk, pray, sing, and bless God.

A Quick Review of Our Anchor Verse

Prompted by the Holy Spirit, Paul prayed this powerful prayer: "And the very God of peace sanctify you wholly; and I pray God your whole spirit and soul and body be preserved blameless unto the coming of our Lord Jesus Christ" (1 Thessalonians 5:23). In this verse, Paul said the three major components of our being are *spirit*, *soul*, and *body*. And it is no coincidence the *spirit* is listed first because it is the deepest part and life force of who we are.

As we saw in Lesson 1, Jesus talked about the need to be *born again* in His conversation with Nicodemus. When the Holy Spirit moves upon us and births us into the family of God, our human spirit is reborn from above. In that moment, our spirit is instantly transformed into the likeness of Christ, and we become just like Him. That is, our spirit is free of all defects, and we are clothed in the righteousness of God (*see* 2 Corinthians 5:21).

The Spiritual Rebirth in Christ
Is Available to Anyone Who Receives It by Faith

In addition to Jesus' conversation with Nicodemus in John 3, we also learn about the spiritual birth from above in John 1. Here, John wrote, "But as many as received him, to them gave he power to become the sons of God, even to them that believe on his name" (John 1:12).

Notice the verse begins with the word "but." This is the Greek word *de*, and here it serves as an exclamatory statement that's intended to get our attention. It's as if John said, "But here this! As many as received Him, to them gave He power to become the sons of God...." The words "as many" in Greek literally means *as great as* or *as much as*. It indicates *an unlimited number* and offers a wide-open invitation to as many as will receive Jesus.

This word "received" is a form of the Greek word *lambano*, which means *to seize or lay hold of something in order to make it your own*. It could also be translated *to grab*; *to capture*; or *to take possession*. It depicts *one who graciously receives something that is freely and easily given*. The use of this word *lambano* signifies that salvation through Christ is freely given to us by God, but to experience it, we must choose to reach out in faith and seize it and make it our own.

Through Faith in Jesus
We Become God's Sons and Daughters

For all those who grab hold of salvation in Christ, He gives "power." This word is a translation of the Greek word *exousia*, which describes *influence* and *delegated authority*. The use of this word means the moment your human spirit is born again, you have been given a new status and have entered a new influence with God and man. God gives you delegated authority "to become a son or daughter of God."

The words "to become" are a form of the Greek word *ginomai*, which here describes *an initiated change that leads to a transition of one thing to another*. The use of the word *ginomai* means being born again is just the beginning, and from that defining moment forward, you're going to grow in your salvation. That initiated change enables you to keep becoming more and more mature as one of God's *sons*.

This word "sons" is the Greek word *teknon*, and it describes *children who are still under parental guidance at home* or *children under the authority of a guardian*. The use of this word tells us that the moment your human spirit is born again, you move into God's house, and He begins to guard and guide you as a loving Father.

John says this loving care is given "…even to them that believe on his name" (John 1:12). In Greek, the word "on" is the remarkable word *eis*, which would better be translated as *into* and carries the idea of *a merger*. In this case, it is *a divine merger that takes place between you and Jesus* the moment you are born again and call Him Lord.

God Purposely Chose To Birth You Into His Family

Looking at John 1:13, we get an even more detailed picture of what takes place at salvation. The Bible says that we "…were born, not of blood, nor of the will of the flesh, nor of the will of man, but of God [were born]." This verse parallels what we saw in John 3:5 and 6, where Jesus said, "…Except a man be born of water and of the Spirit, he cannot enter into the kingdom of God. That which is born of the flesh is flesh; and that which is born of the Spirit is spirit."

The first birth is the natural birth in which we are born of water by the will of man. It is flesh giving birth to flesh. The second birth is the spiritual birth where our spirit is made alive in Christ. We are born again of the Spirit from above, and it is by the will of God, not man. To enter the Kingdom of God, we must experience this second birth by the Spirit. That is, our human spirit must be supernaturally regenerated by the power of the Holy Spirit.

In First Corinthians 6:17, the apostle Paul said, "But he that is joined unto the Lord is one spirit." The word "joined" here is the Greek word *kollom-enos*, which means *being joined* and carries the idea of one that *is adhering to*, *is cleaving to*, *is joining to*, or *is being glued to*. In this case, the person is being united to the Lord and becoming "one spirit." This phrase is a translation of the Greek words *hen pneuma estin*, which means *one spirit* or *one with the Lord.* Hence, anyone who repents and invites Jesus to be their Lord and Savior becomes inseparably connected with Him.

In Christ, You Are a 'New Creature'

In Second Corinthians 5:17, Paul went on to say, "Therefore if any man be in Christ, he is a new creature: old things are passed away; behold, all things are become new." There is much to be learned from this verse, including the meaning of the words "in Christ." This is a translation of the Greek words *en Christo*, which literally means, *in Christ* or *located in Christ* or *in the sphere of Christ.*

Anyone who has been placed in the sphere of Christ is a "new creature." The word "new" here is a form of the Greek word *kainos*, and it describes *something new, brand new,* or *freshly new.* It is not a new version of something old but something *brand spanking new.* In Christ, you are a totally brand-new *creature*, and the word "creature" is a form of the Greek word *ktisis.* This word describes *a creation,* but most importantly, it is *something made from nothing.* Hence, it is not made with old materials, but something that never previously existed. That's who you are in Christ — a brand spanking new creation that is totally different from what you once were.

Paul then said, "…Old things are passed away…" (2 Corinthians 5:17). In Greek, "old things" is *ta archaia,* which refers to *the archaic things; the old things; the past things.* The phrase "passed away" is a translation of the Greek word *parerchomai,* which describes *something passed or rendered void.* We could even translate this word as *null and void.* It means *to be disregarded* or *to be ignored,* and in this verse speaks of *archaic things no longer relevant about your life.*

Along with the old things about you that are null and void, Paul said, "…Behold, all things are become new" (2 Corinthians 5:17). The word "behold" is the Greek word *idou,* which is a term that carries the idea of *bewilderment, shock, amazement,* and *wonder.* It's use here is the equivalent of Paul saying, "Wow! It's so amazing how all things become new!" Once more we see the word "new" — a form of the Greek word *kainos* — describing something *brand new* or *freshly new,* not a new version of something old, but *brand spanking new.*

Our Spirit Is Made Brand New
and Its Home Is Our Body

As we've noted, it is our spirit that experiences total regeneration at salvation. When you're born again, you know it because the Holy Spirit enters your human spirit and brings it back to life! This is confirmed in Romans 8:16 (*ESV*), which says, "The Spirit himself bears witness with our *spirit* that we are children of God." When you repent of sin and surrender your life to Jesus, your human spirit that was dead in sin is instantly born again and placed in Christ Jesus (*see* Ephesians 2:1). Suddenly, the Holy Spirit begins communicating and confirming with your spirit that you are a child of God, and you have an internal knowing that you're saved and belong to Him.

Now, your soul and body remain the same — they don't change at salvation. It's only your spirit man — the life force of your being — that is made brand spanking new. Remember, the Bible says, "…The body apart from the spirit is dead" (James 2:26 *ESV*). When the human spirit leaves the body, the body and soul die because your spirit is the life force of your being.

The apostle Paul referred to the moment our spirit leaves our body in Second Corinthians 5:8. Here he declared, "We are confident, I say, and willing rather to be absent from the body, and to be present with the Lord." Interestingly, the word "absent" is the Greek word *ekdemeo*, and it means *to be away from home*. Hence, the human body is the *home* of the human spirit. This is why Kenneth E. Hagin, one of the most profound teachers of God's Word, often said, "I *am* a spirit, I *have* a soul, and I *live* in a body." Indeed, our body is the house for our spirit, and it is the temple of the Holy Spirit (*see* 1 Corinthians 6:19). Although our body is only a temporary container, we need to take care of it, so we can accomplish all that God has called us to do.

What Can Your Spirit Do?

The human spirit, which is the real you, is actually quite extraordinary and can do great things. For instance, your spirit can *pray*. First Corinthians 14:14 says, "For if I pray in an unknown tongue, my spirit prayeth, but my understanding is unfruitful." Here Paul referred to praying in the heavenly language of the spirit. In the original Greek text, this verse says, "For if I pray in an unknown tongue, the spirit of me, my spirit prays.…"

Don't miss this. Your spirit — the deepest part of your being — is able to talk and pray when you pray in tongues. The heavenly language of tongues is literally our human spirit speaking. If you want to become familiar with your human spirit and what's going on inside of you, begin praying in tongues more.

When we pray in the spirit, the Bible says our "…understanding is unfruitful" (1 Corinthians 14:14). To navigate this challenge, Paul said, "…I will pray with the spirit, *and* I will pray with the understanding also: I will sing with the spirit, *and* I will sing with the understanding also" (1 Corinthians 14:15). Again, the original Greek in this passage is quite interesting. The phrase "with the spirit" is *to pneumati*, which means *with the human spirit*, and the phrase "with the understanding" is *to noi* in Greek, meaning *with the human mind, with the intellect*, or *in the language of the mind*. So to experience the greatest benefits from prayer, we are to pray with our human spirit in the unknown language of tongues, and we are also to pray with our human mind with words we understand.

In addition to praying, we are also to *sing*. Paul said, "…I will sing with the spirit, and I will sing with the understanding also" (1 Corinthians 14:15). Here again, the Greek text says this differently. The words "[sing] with the spirit" are a translation of the Greek words *to pneumati*, which mean *with the human spirit*, and the words "[sing] with the understanding" are *to noi* in Greek, which mean *with the human mind, with the intellect*, or *in the language of the mind*. Thus, we can both pray and sing with our spirit.

First Corinthians 14:16 then adds that we can "bless with the spirit." Once more, we see the phrase "with the spirit" — the Greek words *en pneumati* — which mean *in the human spirit* or *in the realm of the human spirit*. So with your human spirit, you can talk and pray to God, sing to God, and bless Him with words of worship. All this comes from your spirit — the real you, the deepest part of who you are where the Spirit of God Himself lives.

Our Spirit Is Renewed Daily

In the New Testament, the human spirit is also referred to as the *inner* or *inward man*. We see this in Second Corinthians 4:16 where Paul wrote, "For which cause we faint not; but though our outward man perish, yet the inward man is renewed day by day." The phrase "outward man" is a translation of the Greek words *ho exo hemon anthropos*, which describes *the exterior man, our exterior self*, or *the human body*. Paul stated that our outward man or human body is *perishing*, and that word "perish" is the Greek word *diaphtheiro*, which means *to suffer the effects of wear, tear, and age*.

Clearly, no one would argue that our physical bodies are bombarded daily with the effects of wear, tear, and age. The good news is that "…the inward man is renewed day by day" (2 Corinthians 4:16). In Greek, the phrase "inward man" is a translation of the words *ho eso hemon*, which describe *the inner part of us*. The Bible states that day by day our born-again human spirit is being "renewed." In Greek, the word "renewed" is *anakainoo*, which means *renewed again and again*. Hence, it is *endlessly fresh, new*, and *unaffected by the effects of wear, tear*, and *age*! Wow! Praise God for that!

Friend, the moment you were born again, your spirit was born from above by the Spirit of God, and you became one with the Lord. When you surrendered to Jesus, you were joined to Him and became glued together with Him in the Spirit. He entered your human spirit through the Person of the Holy Spirit, and your human spirit was created brand spanking new.

In that instant, your spirit was declared righteous and made perfect in Christ — free of all defects. Through your born-again spirit, you can communicate with God — you can talk, pray, and sing to Him — and even bless Him in worship. Filled with the power of God, your human spirit is not subject to wear, tear, and age. As you get older, your human spirit continues to reach a higher and more advanced status.

In our next lesson, we will turn our attention to the mind, which is the control center of our life.

STUDY QUESTIONS

> **Study to shew thyself approved unto God, a workman that**
> **needeth not to be ashamed, rightly dividing the word of truth.**
> **— 2 Timothy 2:15**

1. John 1:12 says, "But as many as received him, to them gave he power to become the sons of God, even to them that believe on his name." What does the Bible say about being a son or daughter of God? Reflect on these powerful promises:

    • What does being a child of God demonstrate?
    (*See* First John 3:1 and 2.)

- What do sons and daughters of God do?
  (*See* Matthew 5:9 and Philippians 2:15.)

- What Gift does God give His children?
  What does that Gift enable them to do?
  (*See* Romans 8:14-16 and Galatians 4:6.)

2. According to First Corinthians 14:14-16, what things can you do with your human spirit? Did you know your spirit had all these capabilities? What is most surprising about this passage?

3. What does the Bible say happens when you pray in tongues, the language of the spirit? (*See* First Corinthians 14:4 and Jude 20.) How often and for what reason should you pray in the spirit? (*See* Ephesians 6:18; and Romans 8:26 and 27.)

PRACTICAL APPLICATION

> But be ye doers of the word, and not hearers only,
> deceiving your own selves.
> —James 1:22

1. Romans 8:16 (*ESV*) says, "The Spirit himself bears witness with our spirit that we are children of God." Have you sensed the Holy Spirit communicate and confirm with your spirit that you are a child of God? How would you describe this internal knowing that you're saved and belong to Him?

2. Being born again is just the beginning of our new life in Christ. From that moment forward, we are to continue growing in our salvation. What evidence in your life shows that you are growing and maturing as a believer? What is something you really struggled with when you first got saved that you don't struggle with any longer?

TOPIC

The Mind: The Central Control Center of Your Life

SCRIPTURES

1. **1 Thessalonians 5:23** — And the very God of peace sanctify you wholly; and I pray God your whole spirit and soul and body be preserved blameless unto the coming of our Lord Jesus Christ.

2. **Romans 12:2** — And be not conformed to this world: but be ye transformed by the renewing of your mind, that ye may prove what is that good, and acceptable, and perfect, will of God.

3. **Ephesians 4:23** — And be renewed in the spirit of your mind.

4. **Colossians 3:10** — And have put on the new man, which is renewed in knowledge after the image of him that created him.

5. **James 1:21** — Wherefore lay apart all filthiness and superfluity of naughtiness, and receive with meekness the engrafted word, which is able to save your souls.

6. **2 Peter 1:2** — Grace and peace be multiplied unto you through the knowledge of God, and of Jesus our Lord.

GREEK WORDS

1. "sanctify" — **ἁγιάζω** (*hagiadzo*): to sanctify, to set apart, or to consecrate as holy

2. "wholly" — **ὁλοτελής** (*holoteles*): a compound of **ὅλος** (*holos*) and **τέλος** (*telos*); the word **ὅλος** (*holos*) means every single part and pictures all the parts working together in sync; the word **τέλος** (*telos*) depicts completion or maturity; compounded, it describes fully layered parts

3. "transformed" — **εταμορφόω** (*metamorphoo*): the word **μετά** (*meta*) and **μορφόω** (*morphoo*); the word **μετά** (*meta*) means a turn or a change; the word **μορφόω** (*morphoo*) depicts a shape, form, or essence; to change or to turn into a new shape, form, or essence; in this verse, it pictures a mind that is in the process of transformation

4. "renewing" — ἀνακαίνωσις (*anakainosis*): the act of making new again; to put back into its original condition before it was spoiled; to renovate; a complete renewal or restoration

5. "mind" — νοῦς (*nous*): the mind; it refers to the ability to think, to reason, to understand, and to comprehend; the place from which one rules and controls his inward and outward environment; the central control center for a human being; the place where reasoning, perception, and understanding take place

6. "renewed" — ἀνανεόω (*ananeoo*): a compound of the preposition ἀνά (*ana*) and νέος (*neos*); the preposition ἀνά (*ana*) means again, while the word νέος (*neos*) depicts what is fresh, new, or young; hence, to put back into the intended original condition; the preposition ἀνά (*ana*) also means upward, thus, leading the mind to an advanced and higher state of being

7. "renewed" — ἀνακαινόω (*anakainoo*): renewed again and again; hence, endlessly fresh, new, and unaffected by the effects of wear, tear, and age

8. "in knowledge" — ἐπίγνωσις (*epignosis*): a well-instructed, intensive, deep knowledge of the facts; it pictures one who knows his facts like a professional; very knowledgeable

9. "receive" — δέχομαι (*dechomai*): to take quickly, to take readily, or to take with a receptive and welcoming attitude

10. "meekness" — πραΰτης (*prautes*): a strong-willed person who has learned to submit his will to a higher authority

11. "engrafted" — ἔμφυτος (*emphutos*): engrafted; subsequently implanted

12. "save" — σῴζω (*sodzo*): delivering and healing power; to deliver, heal, preserve, or protect

13. "souls" — ψυχή (*psuche*): mind, will, and emotions

14. "multiplied" — πληθύνω (*plethuno*): to amplify, to make full, to increase, to maximize, or to multiply; hence, to multiply and proliferate until they abundantly overflow

15. "through" — ἐν (*en*): the preposition ἐν (*en*) means in, inside, in the sphere, or in the realm; it can be translated in, as in the sphere where this act occurred, or by, as in the agency by which it occurred; this verse emphatically declares that as believers continuously grow in their knowledge of the Lord Jesus Christ, grace and peace are multiplied in their lives

16. "the knowledge" — ἐπίγνωσις (*epignosis*): a compound of the preposition ἐπί (*epi*) and γινώσκω (*ginosko*); the preposition ἐπί (*epi*) here is an intensifier and means on or upon, as in being on top of something, and the word γινώσκω (*ginosko*) means I know, I perceive, I realize, or I recognize and carries the idea of knowing something by experience; compounded as a single word, it pictures experiential knowledge, first-hand knowledge, personal knowledge, or one who is expertly on top of his subject; it depicts obtaining masterful knowledge until one becomes a top-notch expert

SYNOPSIS

As we've seen in our first two lessons, Russian Matryoshka dolls have been a sought-after item for many years. These multi-layered collectibles are hand carved, hand painted, and come in a wide variety of shapes and sizes. Over time, they have even taken on the form of famous political figures. That's right — from Khrushchev to Gorbachev and from Lenin to Stalin, these nesting dolls are quite whimsical indeed.

And just as these figurines are made of multiple layers, we, too, have multiple parts. The Bible says that we are a spirit, we have a soul, and we live in a body, and God wants us to surrender every part of who we are to Him. Although our spirit — the innermost part of our being — is totally made new and perfect the moment we're saved, our soul and body still need a great deal of work. The key to experiencing regeneration in these outer layers is in learning to renew our mind with God's Word.

The emphasis of this lesson:

Although our spirit is instantly transformed the moment we're saved, our soul — which includes our thinking — remains unchanged. That's why we're repeatedly told in Scripture to renew our mind. The more we renew our mind with God's Word, the more we will begin to think like Him, talk like Him, believe like Him, and act like Him. Our mind is the control center of our life.

We Are Multi-Layered Beings — Each Part Is Designed To Work Together

Your spirit is the very core of who you are, and it is the life force of your being. Without the spirit, there is no life (*see* James 2:26). When we surrender ourselves to the lordship of Jesus, our human spirit is reborn from above by the Spirit of God, and we become one with Christ. With our spirit, we can communicate with God on the deepest, most intimate level possible. We can talk, pray, sing, and bless the Lord wherever and whenever we want.

In the closing verses of Paul's first letter to the Thessalonians, he said, "And the very God of peace sanctify you wholly; and I pray God your whole spirit and soul and body be preserved blameless unto the coming of our Lord Jesus Christ" (1 Thessalonians 5:23). Notice Paul prayed that "…the very God of peace sanctify you wholly…." The word "sanctify" here is the Greek word *hagiadzo*, which means *to sanctify*, *to set apart*, or *to consecrate as holy*. That is what God wants to do in every area of your life, and He wants to do this "wholly."

This word "wholly" is the Greek word *holoteles*, a compound of *holos* and *telos*. The word *holos* means *every single part* and pictures *all the parts working together in sync*. And the word *telos* depicts *completion* or *maturity*. When these words are compounded to form *holoteles* — translated here as "wholly" — it describes *a fully layered being in which all the parts work together in sync*.

That's what we are — fully layered beings. At our very core, we are spirit; the middle layer is a soul, and the outermost layer is a body. What's interesting is that when you read First Thessalonians 5:23 in the Greek text, the words spirit, soul, and body each have a definite article preceding them. It reads *the* spirit, *the* soul, and *the* body. This added emphasis shows that Paul was specifically telling us that we are made of three distinct parts, and the fact that the word *holos* is included shows that God's intention is that all three parts of us function together in sync.

We Are Commanded To
'Renew Our Minds'

While the spirit is instantly reborn at the moment of salvation, the soul remains unchanged. The Greek word for "soul" is *psuche*, and it describes *the mind*, *will*, and *emotions* of a person. Because our soul doesn't instantly change like our spirit, we carry wrong ways of thinking into our new life in Christ. God's objective is to take what has happened in our spirit and allow it to transform our soul, and this is accomplished by *renewing our mind*. God makes this clear in Romans 12:2, where Paul wrote:

And be not conformed to this world: but be ye transformed by the renewing of your mind, that ye may prove what is that good, and acceptable, and perfect, will of God.

The word "transformed" in this verse is the Greek word *metamorphoo*, which is a compound of the words *meta* and *morphoo*. The word *meta* describes *a turn* or *a change*, and the word *morphoo* depicts *a shape, form,* or *essence*. When these words are combined to form *metamorphoo*, it means *to change* or *to turn into a new shape, form, or essence*. In this verse, it pictures a mind that is in the process of transformation. Thus, renewing our mind is not instantaneous; it's a process that takes time.

This brings us to the word "renewing" — the Greek word *anakainosis*. This term describes *the act of making new again* or *putting something back into its original condition before it was spoiled*. It means *to renovate* and depicts *a complete renewal or restoration*. If you think about it, our mind has been greatly corrupted by the world around us. Ungodly media, music, movies, relationships, and our fallen nature have all contributed to warping and perverting our thinking.

The remedy for our mental depravity is to fill our minds with the Word of God. No book on earth has the transforming power of Scripture. As we take God's Word in, it has the extraordinary ability to penetrate deep into our soul and purge us of all the lies and filth that have shaped our thinking. Ephesians 5:26 (*NLT*) says we are "…washed by the cleansing of God's word." Little by little, the truth of Scripture puts our mind back into the original condition that God intended, and we begin to think the way He thinks.

Your Mind Is the Control Center of Your Life

Again, God wants you to be "…transformed by the renewing of your mind…" (Romans 12:2). The word "mind" in this passage is the Greek word *nous*, and it refers to *the mind* or *the ability to think, to reason, to understand,* and *to comprehend*. It is *the place from which one rules and controls his inward and outward environment*. Indeed, the mind is the central control center for a human being — the place where reasoning, perception, and understanding take place.

The reason the mind is called the central control center of your life is because it is a part of the soul, which is present between your spirit and your body. Even though the power of God is living in you, your mind is

like the gatekeeper that decides which part of you is going to dominate —
your spirit or your flesh.

Are you going to be dominated by your human spirit where God lives and
His perfection and power reign? Or is your flesh going to run you around,
acting like a tyrannical dictator that demands to have his way? Again, your
mind is the decisionmaker between your spirit and your flesh, and as the
gatekeeper, it determines the direction of your life.

If your mind is not renewed, it will tend to gravitate toward letting your
flesh have its way. In other words, an unrenewed mind *thinks* what it
wants to think, *says* what it wants to say, and *does* what it wants to do. It
is unbridled, unrestrained, and undisciplined. However, if you renew your
mind and bring it into agreement with your spirit and God's Word, your
mind will give authority to your spirit to lead the way. Consequently, all
the realities of your new life in Christ will begin to dominate your life.
That's why it's so vital that you renew your mind.

Renewing Your Mind *Improves* Your Mind

The practice of renewing our mind is mentioned throughout the New
Testament. For example, Ephesians 4:23 says, "And be renewed in the
spirit of your mind." In this passage, the word "renewed" is the Greek
word *ananeoo*, which is a compound of the preposition *ana* and *neos*. The
preposition *ana* means *again*, while the word *neos* depicts what is *fresh*,
new, or *young*. Hence, when these words are compounded to form *ananeoo*,
it means *to put back into the intended original condition*.

There's something else that's interesting about the preposition *ana*, the
first part of the word "renewed." It also carries the idea of *moving upward*.
Thus, when our mind is being renewed, it is being led to an advanced and
higher state of being.

Many have thought and believed that as you get older, your mind is supposed to deteriorate in its ability. However, if you're renewing your mind
with God's Word, it will not deteriorate. Instead of becoming forgetful,
your mind can stay alive, fresh, and new. In fact, your mind's ability can
even improve. A recent medical report shows that if you consistently use
your mind, it will actually reach its peak performance between 70 and
90 years old. When you add the renewing of your mind to this natural
process, the power of God's Word and the Holy Spirit will enable your
mind to function better the older you get!

Again, the word "mind" in Ephesians 4:23 is the Greek word *nous*, which literally describes *the human mind*. It refers to *the ability to think, reason, understand*, and *comprehend*; it is the place from which one rules and controls his inward and outward environment. When you take time to read, study, and memorize God's Word, the positive results will be amazing. Jesus said, "…The measure [of thought and study] you give [to the truth you hear] will be the measure [of virtue and knowledge] that comes back to you—and more [besides] will be given to you *who hear*" (Mark 4:24 *AMPC*).

The more you renew your mind with God's Word, the more you will come into agreement with His ways. As a result, you will think like Him, talk like Him, believe like Him, and act like Him more and more. Renewing your mind with the Word creates a pipeline between your spirit and mind, allowing all the wisdom of Christ to flow from your spirit into your mind and begin to dominate your thinking and ultimately your body. Are you beginning to see how important it is to renew your mind?

To Put on the New Man
We Must Be Renewed 'In Knowledge'

In addition to Romans 12:2 and Ephesians 4:23, the apostle Paul talked about renewing the mind in Colossians 3:10. In this verse, he said, "…Put on the new man, which is renewed in knowledge after the image of him that created him." The word "renewed" here is the Greek word *anakainoo* — which is different than the Greek word for "renewing" used in Romans 12:2. The word *anakainoo* carries the idea of *being renewed again and again*. Hence, it means *endlessly fresh, new, and unaffected by the effects of wear, tear, and age*.

What's interesting about Colossians 3:10 is that it says the mind is renewed "in knowledge." This phrase is a translation of the remarkable Greek word *epignosis*, a compound of the words *epi* and *ginosko*. Here, the word *epi* serves as an intensifier, and the word *ginosko* depicts *knowledge*. When the two words are compounded to form *epignosis*, it depicts *a well-instructed, intensive, deep knowledge of the facts*. It pictures *one who knows his facts like a professional; one who is very knowledgeable*.

The use of this word *epignosis* — translated here as "in knowledge" — tells us that as we renew our mind with everything the Word of God teaches, we develop a well-instructed, intensive, deep knowledge of the truth. As a result, we become like a professional in our expertise and knowledge of Scripture and gain the ability to rightly divide the Word in any given situation (*see* 2 Timothy 2:15). That's the kind of inherent power the Word of God contains.

God's Word Packs the Power
To Save Your Soul!

Another scripture that illustrates the power of renewing our minds is James 1:21, which says, "Wherefore lay apart all filthiness and superfluity of naughtiness, and receive with meekness the engrafted word, which is able to save your souls." There are several important words to understand in this passage, and the first one we want to look at is the word "receive."

In Greek, the word "receive" is *dechomai*, which means *to take quickly*, *to take readily*, or *to take with a receptive and welcoming attitude*. It is the picture of a person who wastes no time but quickly throws their arms wide open to receive and welcome what God's Word says. Furthermore, this person welcomes and receives the Word with "meekness." Although many have thought that meekness means weakness, it doesn't.

"Meekness" is a translation of the Greek word *prautes*, which is quite unique. It describes *a strong-willed person who has learned to submit his will to a higher authority*. Although this individual once thought he or she was always right, this person has learned by experience that God knows better than he or she does, and therefore, this person now willingly chooses to submit to what His Word says.

Realize that there will be times when your unrenewed mind will argue and disagree with God's Word. When it does, you have to tell it to shut up and obey what the Word says. This mindset of *meekness* — the Greek word *prautes* — is something we must have in order to receive the engrafted Word.

What does the word "engrafted" mean? It is the Greek word *emphutos*, which means *engrafted* or *subsequently implanted*. One of the best illustrations of the meaning of *emphutos* is an *organ transplant*. Can you think of someone who needed a new kidney? A new lung? Or even a new heart? If they received a new organ, that organ had to be *engrafted* into their body. It was not there originally; it was implanted in their body afterward.

Normally, when someone receives a transplanted organ, their body immediately begins to reject it — even though the body needs it to live. To prevent rejection, doctors give the transplant recipient medicine to take every day for the rest of their life so the body will receive the organ and, ultimately, save their life.

In the same way, when God's Word comes to us, our soul — which is our *mind, will,* and *emotions* — often automatically rejects what it says. When that happens, we must choose to receive the engrafted Word with meekness because it has the power to "…save [our] souls" (James 1:21). The word "save" here is the Greek word *sodzo,* and it describes *delivering and healing power.* It is a supernatural ability *to deliver, heal, preserve,* or *protect.*

What is the Word of God *delivering, healing, preserving,* and *protecting*? The Bible says our "souls," which is the Greek word *psuche,* describing our *mind, will,* and *emotions.* Our "soul" is the problem. Apart from God, it doesn't think right, it's misled by wrong feelings, and ends up making wrong decisions. Therefore, just like a person with a bad organ needs to receive an organ transplant, we must receive the engrafted Word of God because it is the only thing that has the power to prolong our life and deliver us from wrong thinking, faulty feelings, and ungodly decisions.

Renewing Your Mind
Multiplies God's Grace and Peace to You

The more you submit your mind to the Word of God and come into agreement with the new ideals He has deposited in your spirit, the more you will think the way God thinks. This is what it means to have "the mind of Christ" (*see* 1 Corinthians 2:16). Second Peter 1:2 says, "Grace and peace be multiplied unto you through the knowledge of God, and of Jesus our Lord." What happens when your mind is renewed with the truth of God's Word? Grace and peace are multiplied to you!

The word "multiplied" in this verse is the Greek word *plethuno,* which means *to amplify, make full, increase, maximize,* or *multiply.* It also means *to proliferate until they abundantly overflow.* Again, grace and peace are multiplied and overflow to you "…through the knowledge of God, and of Jesus our Lord" (2 Peter 1:2).

In Greek, the word "through" is the little word *en,* which is a preposition that means *in, inside, in the sphere,* or *in the realm.* It can be translated "in," as *in the sphere where this act occurred,* or "by," as *in the agency by which it occurred.* This verse emphatically declares that as believers continuously grow in their knowledge of the Lord Jesus Christ, grace and peace are multiplied in their lives.

So what do the words "the knowledge" mean? Once again, it is the Greek word *epignosis*, a compound of the preposition *epi* and the word *ginosko*. The word *epi* is an intensifier and means *on* or *upon*, as in being *on top of something*. And the word *ginosko* means *I know, I perceive, I realize,* or *I recognize*, and it carries the idea of *knowing something by experience*. When compounded as a single word, *epignosis* pictures *experiential knowledge, first-hand knowledge, personal knowledge,* or *one who is expertly on top of his subject*. It depicts obtaining masterful knowledge until one becomes a top-notch expert.

Essentially, what Peter was telling us in this verse is that as we submit our minds to the Word of God and really become top-notch experts in the knowledge of Jesus, and the Word of God floods our mind, our mind is renewed and gets into agreement with what God has already done in our spirits through the work of salvation.

It then throws open the door for all the rich treasures of Christ to flow from our spirit and into our mind. We then become actual participants who experience God's divine nature in our life (*see* 2 Peter 1:4). Almost seamlessly, our mind begins to decide we're going to be dominated by our spirit, and our body becomes our instrument or tool to do what's right rather than a dominating instrument to do evil.

STUDY QUESTIONS

> **Study to shew thyself approved unto God, a workman that needeth not to be ashamed, rightly dividing the word of truth.**
> **— 2 Timothy 2:15**

1. When you take time to read, study, and memorize God's Word, the positive results are amazing! According to these verses, what can you expect to happen in your life as you regularly feed on the truth of Scripture?

   • Psalm 119:9,11,105

   • Jeremiah 15:16 and Psalm 119:103

   • Acts 20:32

   • 1 Peter 2:2

- Romans 1:16 and James 1:21

- 2 Timothy 3:16,17

2. God's Word is the greatest gift we've been given for renewing our mind, and few scriptures describe what the Word does like Hebrews 4:12. Take time to meditate on this amazing verse in the *Amplified Classic* version, and jot down what the Holy Spirit reveals to you about the transforming power of Scripture.

   For the Word that God speaks is alive and full of power [making it active, operative, energizing, and effective]; it is sharper than any two-edged sword, penetrating to the dividing line of the breath of life (soul) and [the immortal] spirit, and of joints and marrow [of the deepest parts of our nature], exposing and sifting and analyzing and judging the very thoughts and purposes of the heart.

3. The unrenewed mind is what the Bible calls *the mind of the flesh*, and the renewed mind is *the mind of the Spirit*. Take time to carefully read through Romans 8:5-13 and identify the stark differences between these two mindsets. What is the Holy Spirit revealing to you in this passage?

PRACTICAL APPLICATION

> But be ye doers of the word, and not hearers only,
> deceiving your own selves.
> —James 1:22

1. In this lesson, we examined several passages about renewing the mind, including Romans 12:2; Ephesians 4:23; Colossians 3:10; James 1:21; and Second Peter 1:2. Out of all these verses and their meanings, which one made the greatest impression on you? Why is this?

2. The Bible says to "…receive with meekness the engrafted word [of God], which is able to save your souls" (James 1:21). In your own words, describe what this verse is saying. How does the original meaning of the words in this passage change your view of reading and studying God's Word?

3. Are you actively renewing your mind with God's Word? If so, how? If not, what's keeping you from it? Pray and ask the Holy Spirit to help

you identify and remove any hindrances that are preventing you from saturating your soul with the greatest book available to man.

TOPIC

The Body: The House Where You Live, the Instrument God Gave You

SCRIPTURES

1. **1 Thessalonians 5:23** — And the very God of peace sanctify you wholly; and I pray God your whole spirit and soul and body be preserved blameless unto the coming of our Lord Jesus Christ.

2. **2 Corinthians 5:6** (*ESV*) — …We know that while we are at home in the body….

3. **2 Peter 1:14** — Knowing that shortly I must put off this my tabernacle, even as our Lord Jesus Christ hath shewed me.

4. **1 Corinthians 6:19,20** — What? know ye not that your body is the temple of the Holy Ghost which is in you, which ye have of God, and ye are not your own? For ye are bought with a price: therefore glorify God in your body, and in your spirit, which are God's.

5. **Romans 12:1** — I beseech you therefore, brethren, by the mercies of God, that ye present your bodies a living sacrifice, holy, acceptable unto God, which is your reasonable service.

6. **Romans 6:12,13** — Let not sin therefore reign in your mortal body, that ye should obey it in the lusts thereof. Neither yield ye your members as instruments of unrighteousness unto sin: but yield yourselves unto God, as those that are alive from the dead, and your members as instruments of righteousness unto God.

7. **1 Thessalonians 4:4** — That every one of you should know how to possess his vessel in sanctification and honour.

GREEK WORDS

1. "sanctify" — **ἁγιάζω** (*hagiadzo*): to sanctify, to set apart, or to consecrate as holy

2. "wholly" — **ὁλοτελής** (*holoteles*): a compound of **ὅλος** (*holos*) and **τέλος** (*telos*); the word **ὅλος** (*holos*) means every single part and pictures all the parts working together in sync; the word **τέλος** (*telos*) depicts completion or maturity; compounded, it describes fully layered parts

3. "whole" — **ὁλόκληρος** (*holokleros*): a compound of **ὅλος** (*holos*) and **κλῆρος** (*kleros*); the word **ὅλος** (*holos*) means every single part and pictures all the parts working together in sync; the word **κλῆρος** (*kleros*) is the word for an inheritance or what is assigned to a person; compounded, it refers to what is assigned and given to each person; complete, entire, or whole in all respects

4. "spirit" — **τὸ πνεῦμα** (*to pneuma*): with a definite article, the spirit; the life force of a person; one's core; one's real self; the eternal part of a person

5. "soul" — **ἡ ψυχὴ** (*he psuche*): with a definite article, the soul; the mind, will, and emotions; the mind is the control center; where we get the words psyche and psychology

6. "body" — **τὸ σῶμα** (*to soma*): with a definite article, the body; refers to the human body

7. "home" — **ἐνδημέω** (*endemeo*): to live in one's own home

8. "tabernacle" — **σκήνωμα** (*skenoma*): a term that describes a tent in which one is temporarily encamped; Peter used this word figuratively to describe his human body, and then went on to state that he would soon be laying aside his body or temporary dwelling place; a temporary tent

9. "temple" — **ναός** (*naos*): a temple or a highly decorated shrine; the image of vaulted ceilings, marble, granite, gold, silver, and highly decorated ornamentation; the most sacred, innermost part of a temple; the holy of holies

10. "beseech" — **παρακαλέω** (*parakaleo*): to urge, beseech, plead, beg, or pray; depicts military leaders who came alongside their troops to urge, exhort, beseech, beg, and plead with them to stand tall and face their battles bravely; to earnestly beg; denotes a word of prayer

11. "present" — **παρίστημι** (*paristemi*): to place at one's disposal; to
    surrender; to offer as a sacrifice to God; to present as a special offer-
    ing to God; to dedicate; used in Luke 2:22 to describe the moment
    when Joseph and Mary presented Jesus to God and dedicated Him in
    the Temple; to fully dedicate with no intention of ever taking it back
    again

12. "yield" — **παρίστημι** (*paristemi*): to place at one's disposal; to surren-
    der; to offer as a sacrifice to God; to present as a special offering to
    God; to dedicate; used in Luke 2:22 to describe the moment when
    Joseph and Mary presented Jesus to God and dedicated Him in the
    Temple; to fully dedicate with no intention of ever taking it back
    again

13. "instruments" — **ὅπλα** (*hopla*): a tool; a weapon

14. "unrighteousness" — **ἀδικία** (*adikia*): unrighteousness; injustice; hurt

15. "know" — **οἶδα** (*oida*): knowledge gained by experience

16. "possess" — **κτάομαι** (*ktaomai*): to control; to manage; to win the
    mastery over

17. "sanctification" — **ἁγιασμός** (*hagiasmos*): that which is consecrated,
    sanctified, or set apart for God's use

18. "honor" — **τιμή** (*time*): cherished, precious, special, or of high value

SYNOPSIS

If there's one souvenir tourists go to the Russian bazaars to buy, it's the
Matryoshka doll. Whatever your interest, there is likely a doll for you.
These multi-layered nesting dolls are decorated in so many styles. Some
are embellished as famous churches or cathedrals, others are painted to
depict familiar fairy tales, and still, others resemble legendary political
figures. You name it, and you can probably find it.

Just as there are multiple layers to these dolls, we, too, are made of multiple layers. We have seen that the deepest part of who we are is our *spirit*. It
is the life force of our being that's instantly born again the moment we're
saved. Our *soul* is the middle layer, and it consists of our *mind*, *will*, and
emotions. The outer layer — the most visible part of who we are — is our
body, and as we'll see in this lesson, it is the house in which the Holy Spirit
takes up residence. Likewise, it is also the instrument through which we
can bring God honor and glory.

The emphasis of this lesson:

Your outer layer, or outward man, is your physical body. It is the temporary tent or home for your spirit and soul and serves as the temple for the Holy Spirit to dwell. We are urged to present our bodies to God as a living sacrifice, which means we are to fully dedicate our body to Him as an instrument of righteousness, having no intentions of ever taking it back.

A Review of Our Anchor Verse
1 Thessalonians 5:23

Looking once more at First Thessalonians 5:23, it says, "And the very God of peace sanctify you wholly; and I pray God your whole spirit and soul and body be preserved blameless unto the coming of our Lord Jesus Christ." There are several key words in this verse that are important to understand.

First, notice Paul prayed that "…the very God of peace will sanctify you wholly." The word "sanctify" here is a form of the Greek word *hagiadzo*, which means *to consecrate*, to sanctify, or *to set apart for God's special use*. Equally important is the word "wholly," which in Greek is the word *holoteles*, a compound of *holos* and *telos*. The word *holos* means *every single part* and pictures *all the parts working together in sync*. The second word *telos* depicts *completion* or *maturity*. When we compound these words to form *holoteles* (wholly), it describes *fully layered beings*, which is what we are.

Paul then added, "…And I pray God your whole spirit and soul and body be preserved blameless unto the coming of our Lord Jesus Christ" (1 Thessalonians 5:23). The word "whole" is similar to the word *wholly*, but here it's the Greek word *holokleros*, a compound of *holos* and *kleros*. The word *holos*, again, means *every single part* and pictures *all the parts working together in sync*, and the second word *kleros* is the word for *an inheritance* or *what is assigned to a person*. When we compound *holos* and *kleros* to form *holokleros*, it refers to *what has been assigned and given to each person by God*, which in context here points to each of us being given a spirit, soul, and body.

When we read First Thessalonians 5:23 in the Greek text, Paul includes *a definite article* when describing each part of who we are. He talks about…

- **The "spirit"** — *to pneuma* in Greek, meaning *THE spirit*, which is the life force of who we are. It is one's core, one's real self, and the eternal part of a person.

- **The "soul"** — *he psuche* in Greek, meaning *THE soul*, which consists of the mind, will, and emotions. Your mind is the control center of your life.

- **The "body"** — *to soma* in Greek, meaning *THE body*, which refers to the human body.

Knowing that our mind is the control center of our life, our ongoing objective should be to renew our mind with God's Word. As we saturate ourselves regularly in the Scriptures — reading, studying, and memorizing the Word — God's thoughts become our thoughts, and all that He has deposited in our spirit at salvation begins to flow up into and dominate our thinking, eventually influencing and affecting our body.

The Human Body Is Our Temporary Home

Your *body* is the house for your spirit and soul. When God formed you in your mother's womb, He formed your spirit first, which is the core of your being — the *real* you. And around your spirit, God created and wrapped your soul, which is your mind, will, and emotions. This is your middleman and the gatekeeper which decides whether your spirit or your flesh will dominate your life.

The outer layer, or outward man, is your physical body. Again, this is the temporary housing for your spirit and soul, which is confirmed in Second Corinthians 5:6 (*ESV*) where Paul wrote, "So we are always of good courage. We know that while we are at home in the body we are away from the Lord." The word "home" here is the Greek word *endemeo*, which literally means *to live in one's own home*. Right now, the real you — your spirit — lives in your *body*, which is *your own home*. And just as you do your best to take care of the house you and your family live in, you must do your best to take care of and maintain your physical body until your assignment here on earth is completed.

Peter alluded to this in his second letter when he said, "Knowing that shortly I must put off this my tabernacle, even as our Lord Jesus Christ hath shewed me" (2 Peter 1:14). The word "tabernacle" in this verse is the

Greek word *skenoma*, a term that describes *a tent in which one is temporarily encamped*. Peter used this word figuratively to describe his human body, and then went on to state that he would soon be laying aside his body or temporary dwelling place.

The word "tabernacle" — the Greek word *skenoma* — is also the word for *a temporary tent*, which is what your body is. It is like a tent that the real you — your spirit — is temporarily encamped in.

Your Body Is Also God's 'Temple'

Amazingly, your body is also the home for the Spirit of God. The apostle Paul talks about this in First Corinthians 6:19, where he asked the question, "What? know ye not that your body is the temple of the Holy Ghost which is in you, which ye have of God, and ye are not your own?" Once again, just as in First Thessalonians 5:23, we see the word "body" — the Greek word *to soma*. It has a definite article, meaning *THE body*, and refers to the human body as *the temple of the Holy Ghost.*

In Greek, the word "temple" is *naos*, and it describes *a temple* or *a highly decorated shrine.* It is the image of vaulted ceilings, marble, granite, gold, silver, and highly decorated ornamentation. This word is the same word used in the Greek Septuagint to describe the most sacred, innermost part of a temple — the holy of holies. By using this term *naos*, Paul was telling us that our body is like the holy of holies for the Holy Spirit!

In the very next verse, Paul went on to say, "For ye are bought with a price: therefore glorify God in your body, and in your spirit, which are God's" (1 Corinthians 6:20). Notice he differentiates between the body and the spirit. He says you're to glorify God in your human body — that's your house — and you're to glorify Him in your spirit, which is the holy of holies where He lives.

We Are To 'Present' Our Body to God

Paul gave similar instructions regarding the care of our body in his letter to the believers in Rome. Here he said, "I beseech you therefore, brethren, by the mercies of God, that ye present your bodies a living sacrifice, holy, acceptable unto God, which is your reasonable service" (Romans 12:1). Notice he opened his letter with the word "beseech," which is the Greek word *parakaleo*, a compound of the words *para* and *kaleo*. The word *para* means *alongside*, and the word *kaleo* means *to urge, beseech, plead, beg,* or *pray*. The new word *parakaleo* means *to come alongside someone to urge, beseech, plead, beg,* or *pray.*

This word was used to depict military leaders who came alongside their troops to urge, exhort, beseech, beg, and plead with them to stand tall and face their battles bravely. Paul's use of this word here depicts him as a commander, and we are like troops that he is coming alongside to plead with. It's as if he is dropping to his knees, pleading with us, and begging us by the mercies of God to present our bodies as a living sacrifice.

The word "present" is also very important. It is the Greek word *paristemi*, and it means *to place at one's disposal* or *to surrender.* It can also mean *to offer as a sacrifice to God; to present as a special offering to God;* or *to dedicate.* It is the same word used in Luke 2:22 to describe the moment when Joseph and Mary presented Jesus to God and dedicated Him at the Temple. Hence, it means *to fully dedicate with no intention of ever taking it back again.*

So, when Paul said, "I beseech you therefore, brethren, by the mercies of God, that ye present your bodies a living sacrifice…," (Romans 12:1) he's urging us to place our body at God's disposal, to make it a sacrifice, to fully surrender it, to present it to God as a special offering, and to give it to Him as a full dedication with no intention of ever taking it back.

Remember, your body is the house where you live and the temple of the Holy Spirit. Deep inside you is your human spirit, the real you that was made brand-spanking new by God and the perfect work of His Spirit. From your born-again spirit, God wants to operate through your soul, sanctifying it and using your body as an instrument for righteousness.

Our Body Is To Be an 'Instrument of Righteousness'

When we turn to Romans 6:12 and 13, we read these instructions from Paul: "Let not sin therefore reign in your mortal body, that ye should obey it in the lusts thereof. Neither yield ye your members as instruments of unrighteousness unto sin: but yield yourselves unto God, as those that are alive from the dead, and your members as instruments of righteousness unto God."

Immediately, this verse informs us that *our body is an instrument* that can be used for unrighteousness or for righteousness. What we produce will be decided by what we *yield* ourselves to. The word "yield" — which appears twice in verse 13 — is the Greek word *paristemi*. It's the same word translated as "present" in Romans 12:1. Again, *paristemi* — translated here as "yield" — means *to place at one's disposal* or *to surrender*. It also means *to offer as a sacrifice to God*; *to present as a special offering to God*; or *to dedicate*. It's the same word used in Luke 2:22 to describe when Joseph and Mary presented Jesus to God and dedicated Him in the Temple.

Paul's use of this word *paristemi* — translated here as "yield" — signifies that we are to *fully dedicate our body to God as His instrument with no intention of ever taking it back again*. The word "instruments," which appears twice in Romans 6:13, is the Greek word *hopla*, and it describes *a tool* or *a weapon*. So, when Paul said, "Neither yield ye your members as instruments of unrighteousness unto sin…" (Romans 6:13), he was saying, "Don't surrender and dedicate your body as a *tool* or *weapon* of unrighteousness…." The word "unrighteousness" is a translation of the Greek word *adikia*, which describes *unrighteousness*, *injustice*, or *hurt*.

Can you think of people who seem to be constantly hurting others? They use their words and actions as deadly weapons to inflict pain and injury in people's lives. This is exactly what God is urging us through Paul not to do. He said, "Don't yield yourself to be a tool or weapon that hurts people and causes injustice. Instead, fully surrender and dedicate yourselves and every part of your body to God to be a tool or weapon that produces righteousness and justice."

Learn To Manage and Control Your Body Honorably

This principle of using one's body for doing right is also seen in First Thessalonians 4:4 where Paul wrote, "That every one of you should know how to possess his vessel in sanctification and honour." The word "know" in this passage is the Greek word *oida*, which describes *knowledge gained by experience*. Thus, this is knowledge learned over time as we walk through experiences.

Moreover, the word "possess" — the Greek word *ktaomai* — means *to control*, *to manage*, or *to win the mastery over*. Hence, this verse is saying that every one of us without exception needs to get some experience and knowledge about how to win the mastery over our *vessel*, which in this case describes the human body. We need to learn how to control it, manage it, and gain the mastery over it in such a way that it is maintained in sanctification and honor.

The word "sanctification" is the Greek word *hagiasmos*, and it describes *that which is consecrated, sanctified*, or *set apart for God's use*. Moreover, the word "honor" — the Greek word *time* — depicts *something cherished, precious, special*, or *of high value.*

Friend, our physical body is precious and highly valued in God's eyes, and we need to do everything we can to consecrate and sanctify it. We are to fully dedicate ourselves into His keeping and not allow our body to become a weapon of unrighteousness or injustice, but a tool of righteousness and justice. The ability to live such dedicated lives is found in continually renewing our minds with the Word of God and allowing the work He's done in our spirit to work through and dominate our soul and body.

STUDY QUESTIONS

Study to shew thyself approved unto God, a workman that needeth not to be ashamed, rightly dividing the word of truth.
— 2 Timothy 2:15

1. Maintaining your body, which is the Holy Spirit's temple, is an ongoing effort that God Himself empowers you to accomplish. According to these verses, what does He repeatedly instruct us to do to remain uncontaminated from sin and the world system?

    - 2 Corinthians 7:1

    - 2 Timothy 2:20-22

    - James 4:8; 1 John 3:3

2. Without question, God longs to be our Father and for us to be His sold-out, set-apart children. What command does He give us in Second Corinthians 6:14-18 regarding our close relationships? How are we to keep ourselves pure?

3. In order to harness your body as an instrument of righteousness, you have to learn to see yourself every day the way that God helped Paul see himself. Carefully read Galatians 2:20; Romans 6:11; and First Corinthians 15:31 and identify this life-giving mindset. (Also consider Jesus' words in Luke 9:23,24 and Paul's words in

Galatians 5:24; Romans 6:6; and Colossians 2:20; 3:3. What is the Holy Spirit showing you in these passages?)

PRACTICAL APPLICATION

> But be ye doers of the word, and not hearers only,
> deceiving your own selves.
> — James 1:22

1. Again and again, the Word of God says that your body is the temple of the Holy Spirit, and He lives in you (*see* 1 Corinthians 3:16; 6:19; 2 Corinthians 6:16; 1 Timothy 1:14; Galatians 4:6; John 14:17; 1 John 2:27; 3:24; 4:13). Why do you think God repeats this truth so many times throughout Scripture? What does this say to you personally about the way you live?

2. God calls us to present or fully dedicate our bodies to Him daily as a living sacrifice. Consider this passage in Romans in *The Message* Bible, and in your own words, describe what you think your life might look like to be a "living sacrifice." How does *renewing your mind* (Romans 12:2) connect with being a living sacrifice?

   So here's what I want you to do, God helping you: Take your everyday, ordinary life — your sleeping, eating, going-to-work, and walking-around life — and place it before God as an offering. Embracing what God does for you is the best thing you can do for him. Don't become so well-adjusted to your culture that you fit into it without even thinking. Instead, fix your attention on God. You'll be changed from the inside out. Readily recognize what he wants from you, and quickly respond to it. Unlike the culture around you, always dragging you down to its level of immaturity, God brings the best out of you, develops well-formed maturity in you.

   — Romans 12:1,2 *MSG*

TOPIC

Let God Touch Every Layer of Your Life

SCRIPTURES

1. **1 Thessalonians 5:23** — And the very God of peace sanctify you wholly; and I pray God your whole spirit and soul and body be preserved blameless unto the coming of our Lord Jesus Christ.

2. **Luke 8:1-3** — And it came to pass afterward, that he went throughout every city and village, preaching and shewing the glad tidings of the kingdom of God: and the twelve were with him, And certain women, which had been healed of evil spirits and infirmities, Mary called Magdalene, out of whom went seven devils, And Joanna the wife of Chuza Herod's steward, and Susanna, and many others, which ministered unto him of their substance.

GREEK WORDS

1. "sanctify" — ἁγιάζω (*hagiadzo*): to sanctify, to set apart, or to consecrate as holy

2. "wholly" — ὁλοτελής (*holoteles*): a compound of ὅλος (*holos*) and τέλος (*telos*); the word ὅλος (*holos*) means every single part and pictures all the parts working together in sync; the word τέλος (*telos*) depicts completion or maturity; compounded, it describes fully layered parts

3. "whole" — ὁλόκληρος (*holokleros*): a compound of ὅλος (*holos*) and κλῆρος (*kleros*); the word ὅλος (*holos*) means every single part and pictures all the parts working together in sync; the word κλῆρος (*kleros*) is the word for an inheritance or what is assigned to a person; compounded, it refers to what is assigned and given to each person; complete, entire, or whole in all respects

4. "spirit" — τὸ πνεῦμα (*to pneuma*): with a definite article, the spirit; the life-force of a person; one's core; one's real self; the eternal part of a person

5. "soul" — ἡ ψυχὴ (*he psuche*): with a definite article, the soul; the mind, will, and emotions; the mind is the control center; where we get the words psyche and psychology

6. "body" — τὸ σῶμα (*to soma*): with a definite article, the body; refers to the human body

7. "healed" — θεραπεύω (*therapeuo*): therapy; carries the idea of repetition; a healing touch that requires corresponding actions

8. "of" — ἀπό (*apo*): away from; separation

9. "evil spirits" — πνευμάτων πονηρῶν (*pneumaton poneron*): spirits of evil; spirits of wickedness; malevolent spirits

10. "infirmities" — ἀσθένεια (*astheneia*): an all-encompassing term for all types of sickness and disease

11. "out of whom" — ἀφ᾽ ἧς (*ap' hes*): from whom; carries the idea of separation

12. "went" — ἐξέρχομαι (*exerchomai*): journeyed out; exited; could have been a process

SYNOPSIS

Throughout this series, we've talked about Matryoshka dolls, which became quite popular in the Nineteenth Century. Over the years, millions of people have purchased these hand-carved, hand-painted keepsakes when visiting Russia. Sometimes referred to as nesting dolls, these whimsical figurines are made up of multiple dolls — one inside the other — and are very diverse in their beauty and uniqueness.

In many ways, we, too, are like Matryoshka dolls — we have many layers and there's more to us than meets the eye. Although we all look very different from one another on the outside, every one of us is a tri-part being consisting of a spirit, soul, and body. God desires to touch and transform every layer of our life — including areas we are not even aware of that need His masterful hand.

The emphasis of this lesson:

The Bible says Jesus *therapied* many people back to health during His earthly ministry, and He's still therapying people back to health today. Mary Magdalene and countless others needed multiple touches from Jesus to be fully healed, and there are times when we, too, need multiple touches from Jesus to be healed in every layer of our life.

God Wants To 'Sanctify You Wholly'

As the apostle Paul concluded his first letter to the believers in Thessalonica, he said, "And the very God of peace sanctify you wholly; and I pray God your whole spirit and soul and body be preserved blameless unto the coming of our Lord Jesus Christ" (1 Thessalonians 5:23).

We've seen that the word "sanctify" is a form of the Greek word *hagiadzo*, which means *to consecrate, to sanctify,* or *to set apart as holy.* Hence, Paul prayed that every part of our being — our spirit, soul, and body — would be consecrated and set apart for God's use. And he asked God to do this "wholly," which is important. This is the Greek word *holoteles*, from the words *holos* and *telos.* The word *holos* means *every single part* and pictures *all the parts working together in sync. Telos,* the second part of the word, describes *what is complete or perfected.* When these words are combined, the new word *holoteles* — translated as "wholly" — depicts *a fully layered being in which every part is working together in sync.*

This verse lets us know that God's plan is for your spirit, soul, and body to work *with* each other — not against each other. Empowered by His sanctifying work, every part of you is to work together in sync and in partnership with one another. That is what this word "wholly" means — to function together as one complete unit.

Everyone Has a *Spirit, Soul,* and *Body*

Paul went on to say, "…And I pray God your whole spirit and soul and body be preserved blameless unto the coming of our Lord Jesus Christ" (1 Thessalonians 5:23). We have noted that the word "whole" in this verse is the Greek word *holokleros*, and although it seems similar to the word *wholly*, it is a bit different. Again, the first part of the word is *holos*, depicting *every single part working together in sync.* But the second part of this word is *kleros*, which describes *an inheritance* or *what has been assigned to a person.*

When these words are compounded to form *holokleros*, it depicts *what has been assigned or given to every single human being on the face of the earth.* In context, this refers to the fact that every human being has been given a spirit, a soul, and a body by God, and in this way we are complete. Indeed, you are a spirit — that's the real you. You have a soul, which is where your mind, will, emotions, and personality reside. And you live in a body.

As we've noted, when we read First Thessalonians 5:23 in the Greek text, Paul included *a definite article* when describing each part of who we are. This shows that each part of us is distinct and separate from the other.

You are a spirit: When Paul talked about our spirit, he said, "THE SPIRIT." This is a translation of the Greek words *to pneuma*, and it describes the life force of who we are — our core, our real self, and the eternal part of being. When a believer in Christ dies, his spirit leaves his body and is immediately present with the Lord (*see* 2 Corinthians 5:8).

You have a soul: When Paul talked about our soul, he said, "THE SOUL." This is a translation of the Greek words *he psuche*, which is where we get the words *psyche* and *psychology*. It describes our mind, will, and emotions — with the mind being the control center of our life.

You live in a body: When Paul talked about our body, he said, "THE BODY." This is a translation of the Greek words *to soma*, and it refers to *the human body*, which is the house in which your spirit and soul live — the instrument God gave you to use to bring Him glory.

What Happened the Moment You Were Saved?

The day you repented of your sin and surrendered your life to Jesus, your spirit was born again from above by the Spirit of God (*see* John 3:3-8). In that moment, your spirit — the real you, the core of who you are — was instantly transformed into the likeness of Jesus.

Although your spirit was made perfect in the new birth, your soul and body remained the same. That is, when you got saved, you didn't walk away from the altar with a new body or a new mind. The transformation of your soul — which includes your mind, will, and emotions — takes time. The Bible calls this process *sanctification*, and it is what Paul referred to in First Thessalonians 5:23 and 24. The transformation of your physical body is what the Bible calls *glorification*, and it will take place at the time of the Rapture or the resurrection (*see* 1 Corinthians 15:42-44; 50-54).

Make no mistake, if you're a believer, your spirit is perfect and righteous like Jesus. If you could see what is inside of you, you would be amazed! In fact, First Corinthians 6:19 says that you are the *temple* of the Holy Spirit. God, the Creator of all that is seen and unseen, lives inside of you in the Person of the Holy Spirit, and the moment you're born again, the Spirit immediately begins to bear witness with your spirit that you are indeed a son or daughter of God (*see* Romans 8:16).

Your Mind Must Be Renewed

Again and again, we are told in Scripture that our mind must be renewed. The fact is, all of us have areas of wrong thinking that developed within us before coming to Christ. We have been mistreated and abused in relationships, we've received varying degrees of wrong modeling from those in authority, and we've also been taught wrong doctrine in church. Thus, we need to renew our minds with the Word of God.

Essentially, the word "renew" means *to restore and put back into the original state that God intended.* As we saturate ourselves in the Scriptures, our minds are washed by the cleansing water of the Word (*see* Ephesians 5:26). The more we feed on and take in God's Word, the more filth and error will be flushed out of our soul. The result is a mind that is constantly being upgraded and refreshed — even into our old age!

Regardless of what many so-called "experts" say, your mind doesn't have to become foggy or forgetful just because you're getting older. If you'll keep renewing your mind with God's Word, it will keep your mind fresh all the way to the end of your life. The Bible says if you receive the Word with meekness — humbly submitting your life to what God says, allowing His truth to become implanted in your heart — it has the power to save your soul (*see* James 1:21). This is why we are told, "And be constantly renewed in the spirit of your mind [having a fresh mental and spiritual attitude]" (Ephesians 4:23 *AMPC*).

If you'll continue to use your mind and renew it with God's Word regularly, your thinking will stay new, fresh, and youthful. Even science now tells us that if you're using your mind consistently, it should reach its most optimum performance between the ages of 70 and 90. And friend, the more you renew your mind with the Word, the more it will come into sync with your spirit, and the more your thinking will be dominated by the Spirit of God living in you.

Instead of your flesh — which is your unrenewed soul and body and all its cravings — dictating how you live, your spirit will be calling the shots. Things like what you think, say, eat, and do will all come under the influence of the Holy Spirit, making you into an instrument of righteousness for God's glory.

People Came to Jesus Multiple Times
Because They Needed Multiple Touches

As we've stated, God wants to touch and transform *every part* of your being — healing and restoring everything about you. This is demonstrated in the way that Jesus most often healed people during His earthly ministry. Consider this passage in Luke 8:1-3:

And it came to pass afterward, that he went throughout every city and village, preaching and shewing the glad tidings of the kingdom of God: and the twelve were with him, And certain women, which had been healed of evil spirits and infirmities, Mary called Magdalene, out of whom went seven devils, And Joanna the wife of Chuza Herod's steward, and Susanna, and many others, which ministered unto him of their substance.

Many people read right over these verses and miss something very important. Looking back at Luke 8:2, it says, "And certain women, which had been healed of evil spirits and infirmities…."The word "healed" in this verse is the Greek word *therapeuo*, which is where we get the word *therapy*. It carries the idea of *repetition* and describes *a healing touch that requires corresponding actions*. Thus, we could say that Jesus *therapied* these women of evil spirits and infirmities.

In Greek, the words "evil spirits" are a translation of the words *pneumaton poneron*, which describes *spirits of evil; spirits of wickedness;* or *malevolent spirits*. And the word "infirmities" is the Greek word *astheneia*, which is an all-encompassing term for *all types of sickness and disease*. The Bible states that Jesus *therapied* these women of the evil, wicked spirits and all types of sickness and disease that beset them. The fact that the word *therapeuo* is used here indicates that some of these women had to come to Jesus multiple times. Apparently, some of the evil spirits were so deeply entrenched that it took multiple touches from Jesus for them to be totally free.

Even the word "of" is important. It is the Greek word *apo*, which means *away from* and describes *a separation*. Jesus *therapied* these women, separating them from and driving away evil spirits and sickness and disease of all kinds. When the Bible talks about Mary Magdalene, "…out of whom went seven devils" (Luke 8:2), the phrase "out of whom" is *ap' hes* in Greek, and like the word "of" (*apo*), it also carries the idea of *separation*.

Keep Bringing Jesus the Broken Areas of Your Life Until Every Layer of Your Life Is Healed

Just as these notable women — and countless others — needed to receive multiple touches from Jesus to experience their full healing, sometimes we too need to receive ongoing ministry from Jesus to be fully healed from what we are dealing with.

As you grow in the Lord, you will likely discover areas in your soul that need healing. These include areas of wrong teaching as well as emotional wounds, and flaws in your thinking that became deeply embedded in you during childhood experiences. As you draw near to the Lord, He will lovingly begin to reveal these unresolved issues and heal you through the washing of the water of His Word (*see* Ephesians 5:26) and the transforming power of His Spirit (*see* 2 Corinthians 3:18).

As long as you're willing to humble yourself and keep bringing Him those parts of yourself that need to be healed, Jesus will continue to *therapy* you back to health. He'll keep releasing His power and peeling back every layer of bondage from your life until, finally, your mind begins to think right and to get in sync with your spirit.

Friend, all the fullness of God is already inside you. It's just not in sync with your mind and your body yet. That's why Paul prayed that your whole spirit, soul, and body would be sanctified and get in sync with the Spirit of God living in you. When all the parts of your being work together as one, suddenly all the treasures of Christ that were deposited in your spirit the day you got saved will begin to flow up into your mind. As a result, your body will become the instrument of righteousness that God intended.

STUDY QUESTIONS

Study to shew thyself approved unto God, a workman that needeth not to be ashamed, rightly dividing the word of truth.
— 2 Timothy 2:15

1. In Matthew 11:28-30, Jesus offers us an invitation without expiration. What does He invite you to do, and what does He promise if you accept His invitation? (Also, consider Jesus' words in Revelation 3:20.)
2. The moment you're born again, God's Seed — First John 3:9 and Second Corinthians 5:17.) As a result, every characteristic of Jesus

now lives in you in *seed form*. Take a few moments to look up and meditate on John 1:16 and Colossians 2:9 and 10 in a few different Bible versions. What extraordinary gift do these verses declare that God has placed in you?

3. Considering the answer to question 2, what are some of the treasures you have full access to through Jesus according to First Corinthians 1:30 and Colossians 2:2,3? (Also, consider Second Peter 1:3,4.)

PRACTICAL APPLICATION

**But be ye doers of the word, and not hearers only,
deceiving your own selves.
— James 1:22**

1. The Bible tells us that Jesus *therapied* many of the people who came to Him for healing. Have you ever been hurt and needed physical therapy to recover? If so, what was the process like? What was injured or broken, and what did the doctor or surgeon do to help restore you physically? What corresponding actions were required of you to experience full recovery?

2. How does this natural process of receiving therapy for your physical body help you better understand the primary way Jesus healed people during His ministry — and the way He's still healing people today?

3. What areas of your soul presently need healing that can only come from Jesus? Where is your thinking out of whack and your heart wounded? In what areas is your will out of alignment with God's will? Take time now to bring these things to God and pray, *Lord, please heal these areas in my life* [name each one specifically]. *I surrender myself to You; tell me what to do, and I'll obey You. Therapy me — heal me completely in these areas of my mind, will, and emotions, in Jesus' name!*

Notes

Notes

CLAIM YOUR FREE RESOURCE!

As a way of introducing you further to the teaching ministry of Rick Renner, we would like to send you FREE of charge his teaching, "How To Receive a Miraculous Touch From God" on CD or USB format.

In His earthly ministry, Jesus commonly healed *all* who were sick of *all* their diseases. In this profound message, learn about the manifold dimensions of Christ's wisdom, goodness, power, and love toward all humanity who came to Him in faith with their needs.

☑ **YES, I want to receive Rick Renner's monthly teaching letter!**

Simply scan the QR code to claim this resource or go to:
renner.org/claim-your-free-offer

R renner.org

f facebook.com/rickrenner • facebook.com/rennerdenise

▶ youtube.com/rennerministries • youtube.com/deniserenner

⊙ instagram.com/rickrrenner • instagram.com/rennerministries_
instagram.com/rennerdenise

www.ingramcontent.com/pod-product-compliance
Lightning Source LLC
Chambersburg PA
CBHW071518030726

47593CB00003B/1317